The To

vvalk

The Tonbridge Knights Walk

in 14 circular walks through the Weald of Kent

by Deborah Cole

ISBN: 978-0-9954752-1-2

First published in 2021

Printed by Biddles Books Ltd

The maps are drawn with permission of the Ordnance Survey, licence number OS100063394

Cover illustrations: a stained glass image, possibly of Gilbert the Red, in Tewkesbury Abbey; with permission of the vicar and churchwardens of Tewkesbury Abbey. Other images are by the author.

Contents

The title of each walk is followed in italics by the corresponding medieval names used on the route description in the medieval manuscript.

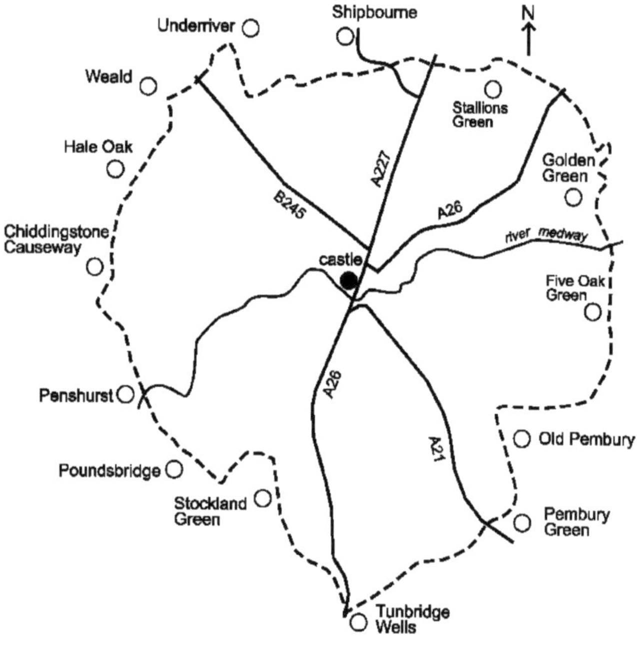

The knights walked in a clockwise direction around Tonbridge, starting near Shipbourne. The dashed line indicates the route and each circular walk passes through the places on the map, in succession.

The Tonbridge Knights Walk

In 1279, a jury of 24 lords and knights walked for 33 miles on what was called *a perambulation of the Lowy of Tonbridge*. The lowy was a circular area stretching for about 4.5 miles in all directions from the castle. It was created to serve the castle, by the first Norman Lord of Tonbridge, Richard Fitzgilbert, founder of the Clare family (Clare after their manor of that name in Suffolk). Some of the land within the lowy had long been disputed, involving the archbishops of Canterbury, bishops of Rochester, the king and others. King Edward I ordered the perambulation (a walk around the perimeter), to investigate the rights of Gilbert the Red, Earl of Gloucester and Lord of Tonbridge at that time. Reports had been flowing in of unlawful occupation and the forcing of tenants both outside and within the lowy, who were exempt, to pay homage and fines to him at court in Tonbridge.

A description of the route, written in medieval Latin, is preserved in Canterbury Cathedral Archives and can be followed, especially as it coincides with many old (pre-1870) parish boundaries. A number of footpaths and minor roads are aligned with the route and have enabled it to be followed closely. This is a new pocket edition of the 2013 publication of *The Tonbridge Circular Walk, in the footsteps of knights*, with updated instructions and offering additional off-road alternatives to the longer road sections, wherever possible.

Walk Notes

This book arranges the 33 mile walk into a series of 14 circular walks ranging from 2-8 miles. They link with each other forming a chain of the whole walk, as well as providing 14 individual pleasant walks in the Wealden countryside. The start points were chosen for ease of parking and the use of public transport. **A B** in the directions mark the section following the knights route and they can be linked for the 33 mile journey. Features of historical interest are written in italics.

Key to Maps

route with direction of travel	**– – – –>**
knights route	**A B**
start point	**S**
alternative route	**- - - - - -**
parish boundary	....

There may be some very muddy or flooded sections in the winter and some fields may have livestock.

Plans can be found at the end of each walk, but OS explorer maps 1:25000 136, 147 and 148 will be helpful in providing greater coverage.

Walk No.1

Shipbourne and Stallions Green

(Somegate to Larkhale)

Distance: 5 miles (4 mile alternative); OS Explorer 147, 148
Start: Shipbourne Green

Old coppiced woods and fields on gentle hills and valleys. A shorter version with less road walking is included.

From the Chaser Inn, cross the A227 to Upper Green Road and take a right diagonal path across the common towards the tree or hedge line, in which there is a gate. Go through and cross the field to Back Lane. Turn left and follow the wide grass verge on the right side of the road. When the verge narrows, turn right through a gate and continue between fields. Turn right and then left around a field and climb up steps. Turn left along a good track through the woods.

A

You are at the beginning of the knights walk, following the edge of the 'northern forest' (North Frith) and part of the large hunting chase of the Clares. The boundary is often marked by many old hornbeam trees, their grey green branches twisting skywards. The fluted bark is a bit like tiger bread. Hornbeam was coppiced and collected as firewoood or made into charcoal to cook with, and to fuel the historic Wealden iron industry. More recently it was used in the oasts for drying hops. Charcoal kilns still operated in the 20th century.

Keep to the main track through the wood, not straying far from the woodland edge. Arrive at Puttenden Lane and cross over to join a footpath on the other side.

Not far left, on this lane, is the hamlet of Claygate. Named on the route, the knights passed this entrance to the northern forest.

Continue along the path to a junction where you can either turn left on the shorter route (with less road), or keep straight on to continue this walk, or join walk 2 (see directions for both routes below).

To the left behind a fence is an old parish boundary stone and ahead of you a boundary bank with footpath on top. Hadlow, in the Lowy of Tonbridge, is on your right while West Peckham is on your left. This part of West Peckham is called Clearhedges and Gilbert the Red unlawfully occupied two mills, a wood and 100 acres, to force it into the lowy, (which he believed to be his right), but was unsuccessful.

Shorter Route:
Turn left just after the boundary stone and continue through the wood, following the footpath signs. You will come closer to the edge of the wood with a large field appearing on your right. When you merge with the field, follow the field edge and then turn right on a main track across the field. Go over a stile and continue down the next field. Continue directions at ****** on page 5.

Continuing Walk 1:
Keep straight until you arrive at a T junction with a wide track. Turn right and next left, on a descending path through the wood. Follow the signs and join a large field, continuing along the left side. Go through a gap to the next field and continue towards a belt of trees ahead. Just before the trees, turn right and follow

a track to High House Lane. Turn left, pass a bungalow and in about 100 metres, pass the footpath on your right to link with Walk 2, otherwise stay on the road.

B

Continue to follow the winding High House Lane and when you reach Three Oaks Cottage on the right, turn next left along a track and shortly go over a stile on your right. Go through a small and then large field, keeping alongside the River Bourne on your right.

****** As you approach the end of the field, cross the river on a footbridge and then turn left through a field with a pylon. Go straight towards a field gate and over the stile to Hamptons Lane. Turn left, continue up the lane and just before a house on your right, turn into the drive and continue ahead along an enclosed path. In about 300 metres, go through a gate on your left and cross the field to Dunks Green Road. Cross over and join the footpath opposite into a field. Continue along the left side to a stile. Climb over and cross the next field to woodland. Go over a stile and a small stream then continue uphill to a field gate. Go over the stile and cross the field to another stile, emerging on School Lane. Cross over and follow the driveway of Fairlawn Home Farm. Negotiate two cattle grids and pass the farm buildings. Continue downhill and then up towards Shipbourne. Continue straight and go through a gate in the field corner to an enclosed track that brings you out on the common. Turn right and continue along the lane to the start of the walk.

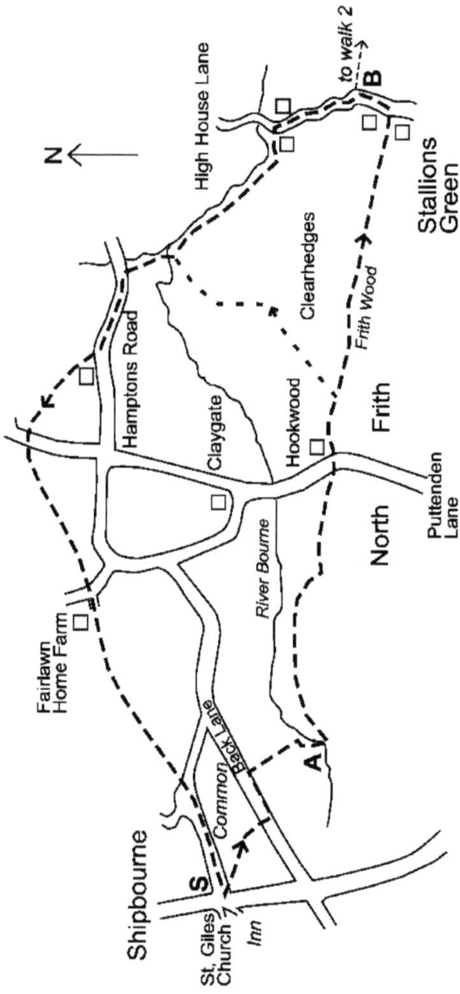
N
High House Lane
to walk 2
B
Stallions Green
Clearhedges
Frith Wood
Hamptons Road
Claygate
Hookwood
Frith
Puttenden Lane
North
River Bourne
Fairlawn Home Farm
Back Lane
Common
A
Shipbourne
S
St, Giles Church
Inn

Walk No.2

Stallions Green and Golden Green

(Larkhale to the kings highway)

Distance: 6.5 miles; OS Explorer 136, 148
Start: Hadlow Village

A mainly level walk through fields and orchards and alongside the River Bourne. Parking is easiest in Hadlow and from here, the walk can be divided into two, both starting and ending where the walk crosses the A26 (see map on page 12).

From Hadlow Square, look for the pelican crossing on the main road and cross over to join a very narrow street called School Lane. Continue as the street narrows to a footpath and cross Hailstone Close. Continue ahead until you come out on Carpenters Lane. Turn right and cross Twyford Road and then Hope Avenue. After Mill View, turn left at a footpath sign and continue down the lane to Bourne Mill.

Cross the yard and go over a footbridge and soon over another footbridge. Fork right and follow the enclosed path with a field on your left. At the end of the field, continue straight and follow the right side of the next field. At the end you will come to a ditch which can be crossed by turning a few metres to the left or by using the stiles or gates on the right. On the other side of the ditch, follow the line of willows as far as the overhead power cables. Look out for a track going off to the right across the field and turn this way, but if it is not clear you can continue to the end of the field and then turn right at the treeline, along a public footpath. Either way, continue until you reach High House Lane. Turn right and pass a bungalow on your left. About 100 metres beyond, look for a footpath on your right at a fieldgate and go over the stile.

A

Continue alongside the right hedge past a pylon. Cross a footbridge over the river Bourne, go across a meadow and over a stile by a fieldgate. Turn right towards a clump of trees.

The trees mark the site of an old moat. It was fashionable for comparatively wealthy people to surround their houses with moats in the late 13th and early 14th centuries.

Continue round the clump and cross a footbridge ahead. Bear left and uphill across the field, towards the far left corner. Hadlow Tower can be seen on your right. The path takes you to a concealed gate in the hedge just before the field corner. Go through the gate to Carpenters Lane. Cross over and turn left along Steers Place in the direction of The Common.

Just before a row of cottages on your right, turn right along a footpath (the sign may be hidden) and enter a field through a gate (if this area is flooded or very muddy, an alternative road route is described below). Keep on the left side of the field and continue in the same direction along an enclosed path to arrive at the A26, Maidstone Road. Cross over to Park View

Cottages and turn right to the last cottage (continue with directions at ** below).

Road Route:
Continue along Steers Place to Common Road. Turn right and continue for about a quarter of a mile to the first footpath on your right. Follow this enclosed path to Valley Drive and turn left to Maidstone Road (A26). Turn right and continue to a row of cottages on your left called Park View Cottages.

** Immediately beyond the last cottage, turn left along a narrow and well concealed footpath. Go across a footbridge and follow a marked path on a zigzag route along the left hedges of a large field. Keep on the lookout for a stile on your left and climb over into an orchard. Follow the footpath straight ahead along the right side of a line of silver birch trees and continue to a gate at the end of the orchard. Go through to Cemetery Lane, turn left and then immediately right into a private road signed 'Bailiff's House', part of Goblands Farm, now a small industrial estate.

Continue between stables and the old engine house. At the end go left for about 200 metres or so, and turn right, following signs, into a field with solar panels. Follow posts along the track ahead and about 100 metres short of a wood bear left and then continue through the wood. Come out onto a track. Turn right and then continue straight across a large field towards houses. Climb over a stile into a sports ground and cross towards a gap in the hedge. Go through and emerge on Bells Farm Lane. Turn right and then left along the next footpath just before Bells Farmhouse. Continue into another field and keep along the right edge to the end of the fence at a path junction. Turn right and join the Weald Way (WW), continuing straight to Hatches Lane. Turn right to a T junction, passing Kent House Farm on your left.

Kent House Farm has a magnificent catslide roof. The name is appropriate for a house on the boundary of the lowy which marks a change in jurisdiction from the sheriff of Kent, representing the king, to the lords of Tonbridge. The name Hatches Lane, meaning opening or gateway, reinforces the notion of a boundary. At the junction, Bells Farm Lane becomes Pierce Mill Lane. In 1279 this road was called 'the king's highway'.

Turn left along 'the kings highway' and continue to the Old Mill. Just before the bridge, turn right through a gateway and keep straight along the left side of a hedge, still following the WW. Continue alongside the river Bourne and cross a footbridge. Soon enter a field and continue in the same direction. Towards the end of the field you will pass a footbridge over the river. Cross only to join Walk 3, otherwise continue on past.

B

Continue alongside the river Bourne on your left. After a while you will arrive at Victoria Road (Golden Green and The Bell Inn, is shortly to the left). Cross over and continue along the south/left bank of the Bourne. Turn right across a footbridge and follow the north bank again. The large building over on the left was once another mill, called Goldhill Mill. Continue alongside the river until you come to a T junction. Turn right and follow the fence on your left. At the end, enter a large field and turn left following the field edge round until you come to a waymarked post.

Turn left here onto a narrow path and follow this widening woodland track for about 200 metres to a concealed gate on your left, set back from the track. Go through the gate and enter a large field where Hadlow Tower is very prominent ahead. Continue on this 'Hadlow Access Trail' and if you are lucky you might find a bench to rest on. At the end of the field go though a gate then keep left. Come out on a modern estate road and bear left to a T junction. Continue straight along a path between houses. Pass St. Mary's Church and turn right along Church Street to Hadlow Square.

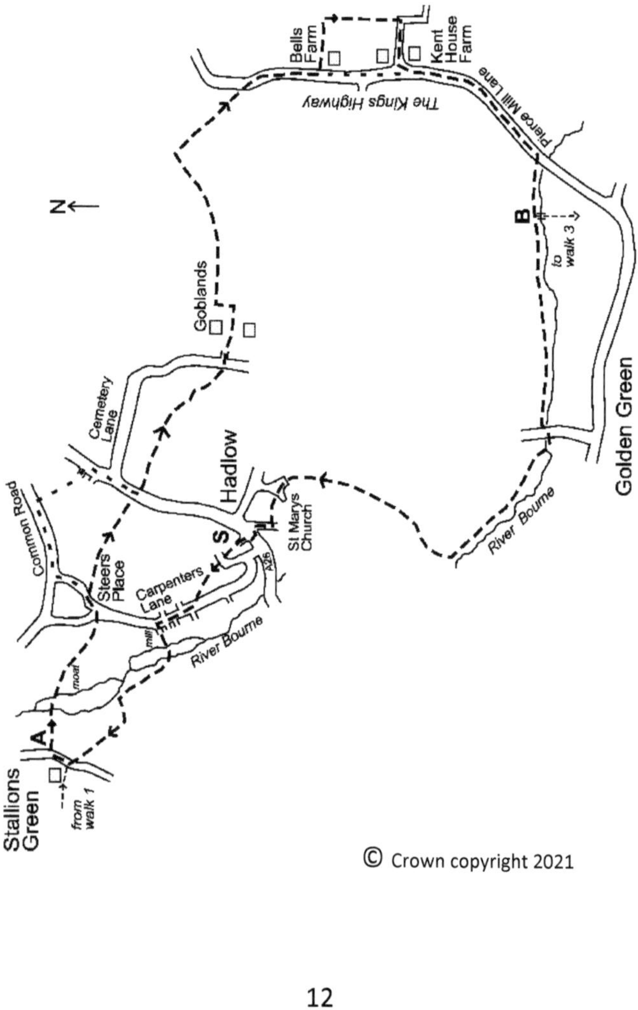
N
Stallions Green
from walk 1
A
moat
River Bourne
mill
Carpenters Lane
Steers Place
Common Road
Cemetery Lane
Hadlow
S
A26
St Marys Church
Goblands
Bells Farm
Kent House Farm
The Kings Highway
Pierce Mill Lane
B
to walk 3
River Bourne
Golden Green

Walk No. 3

Golden Green and Five Oak Green

(the kings highway to wynelingbroke)

Distance: 5 miles or 4.5 shorter alternative; OS Explorer 136
Start: Golden Green (or Five Oak Green, see page 15).

Level walking across the Medway, over large fields, by lakesides and through orchards. An alternative shorter route avoids a long road section at Five Oak Green.

Facing the Bell Inn, turn right along Three Elm Lane, diverting along 'Medway View' to leave the road for a short stretch. After no. 21 Three Elm Lane, turn left along a grassy path and enter a field. Bear right across the field and at the corner, cross over a small stream into another field. Keep left alongside the river Bourne and continue as far as the footbridge but don't cross.

A

Turn sharp right (or keep straight ahead if you have come across the footbridge) and cross the field along the Weald Way (WW). When you reach the opposite boundary there is a choice. Officially, the footpath (WW) crosses a footbridge and stile within the hedge and then bears left to a stile and footbridge within the same hedge, rejoining the field further round. If access is difficult (increasingly the case), save yourself the trouble and turn left along the field edge and continue round to rejoin the footpath. Either way, go through a gate to Barnes Street on Three Elm Lane.

Ahead of you is Barnes Place, a very old house with part said to date from the 13th century.

Turn right and soon (just after The Barn) cross the road and follow a track signed WW. Climb over a stile and continue ahead and then left round the barn. Shortly turn right through a gate and continue alongside a stream. Go through a series of gates and fields, always in the same direction and always with the stream on your left and following the WW, until you arrive at Ford Green Bridge, taking you across the River Medway.

The knights crossed over the river at Oak Weir Lock (cnocewerespole), the next crossing about half a mile downstream. Due to the lack of linking footpaths, your current route was chosen but we will rejoin the knights, for certain, at Pembury Old Church if not before. In this area their route is less distinct but they are never far away.

On the other side of the river, keep straight ahead (south) across the field along a line of trees. About 50 metres before the end of the field, veer right through a wood and at the end, climb over a stile. Continue forward on an enclosed path with a lake soon appearing on your left. Cross a footbridge to a T junction and turn left. Continue, crossing a wide track and then further on, reach a footbridge on your left. Cross over and in about 100 metres at a copse, fork left through a gate. Keep alongside the fence and then cross a wide bridge over a ditch and head straight to

Moat Farm. As you approach, turn left and then right over a footbridge. Turn left and skirt round this large building complex and when you reach a driveway, go across and through a gate ahead.

Turn right along the edge of the orchards, continuing alongside the buildings. Look out for a gap in the tall hedge in front of you, leading on to a driveway. From here a shorter route can be taken, avoiding the road through Five Oak Green. If however, you wish to continue on this route, link with Walk 4 or visit the shop, skip to **Continuing Walk 3**.

Shorter Route:
Continue straight across the driveway, then past the buildings on your right, and then through orchards. At the end, bear right to a footbridge. Cross over and continue to a path junction half way across a field. Turn right and rejoin the route at ** on the next page.

Continuing Walk 3:
Turn left along the drive and continue to the junction with Whetsted Road. Turn right over the railway bridge and continue to Five Oak Green Road. The shop is opposite and shortly to the right of the shop is the link with Walk 4.

B

Turn right along Five Oak Green Road passing 'The Hoppers'.

The Hoppers was once a community hub and a hospital for the hop-pickers who used to arrive each summer, mainly by train from London.

Continue past Oak Road and Larkfield and then turn right into a drive at the next footpath sign, opposite Sychem Lane. Follow the drive for about 400 metres and turn left around old farm buildings and arrive at an area of hoppers huts. Keep left around the huts and then bear right towards a railway bridge. Go through and continue ahead across a long field. Go through a gateway into another field and continue straight.

****** Cross a wide bridge over a ditch to another field and soon follow a long straight ditch on your right, crossing more fields. Cross a plank bridge in a field corner and continue straight ahead, leaving the ditch you have been following. Soon go up a small bank and across a wide bridge over another ditch and bear right alongside the ditch. At the end of the ditch, turn left and cross over the footbridge ahead. Continue between two lakes.

Cross another footbridge and keep ahead across the middle of a field. Go over another footbridge, cross another field and then a short field to a gate leading to East Lock on the Medway.

Go through and cross over the three bridges to the other side. Turn left and then right between two pill boxes on a good track. When this wide track bends noticably left, turn right along a well trodden footpath and continue in the direction of Hadlow Tower, now in view. Go through a gap in the hedge, cross a field straight ahead and merge with a line of poplars along the left side. Continue along the field edge to a gate and go through to Kelchers Lane. Continue along the lane to Golden Green.

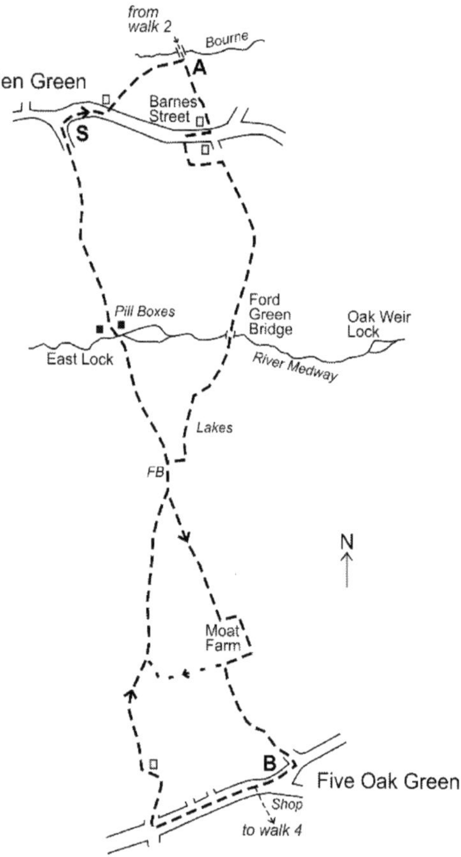
from walk 2
Bourne
A
Golden Green
Barnes Street
S
Ford Green Bridge
Pill Boxes
Oak Weir Lock
East Lock
River Medway
Lakes
FB
N
Moat Farm
B
Five Oak Green
Shop
to walk 4

Walk No. 4

Five Oak Green and Old Pembury

(wynelingbroke to the pale of the forest)

Distance: 4.5 miles; OS Explorer 136.
Start: village hall car park, Falmouth Place, Five Oak Green

A hilly walk with two interesting churches, apple and cherry orchards and woods full of bluebells and wild garlic in spring.

From the car park, turn left along Falmouth Place and then right on a pedestrian path. Emerge on Five Oak Green Road and cross over to the shop.

A

Continue past the shop and shortly look out for a footpath on your left through an arch between Ivy House and Box Cottage. Turn left here and continue along a narrow path to a footbridge. Cross over and keep alongside the stream now on your left.

Alders Stream on your left may be the wyneling brook followed by the knights. They were heading uphill towards the forest pale of Southfrith at Old Pembury.

Keep left at a path fork and continue past an oast house on your right. Go straight across a drive and then left to continue along this winding path between buildings. Cross two footbridges to a hop field and keep on the right side. Look out shortly for a stile on your right. Climb over and cross over a footbridge. Continue on the winding path which crosses a track and narrows. Go through a gate into a field and follow the hedgeline on the right. Keep with the hedge as it curves round and at the end, turn left through a gate. Continue and go through another gate into another field. Head across this next field on a straight course and go through a gate onto Alders Road.

Cross over and climb over a stile opposite. Follow the right side of the field past a bungalow then bear left to a wood along the fenceline. Continue straight on through the wood and veer slightly right towards the gate of an orchard ahead. Go through and keep along the right fenceline uphill and then continue straight ahead to a hedgeline. Bear left alongside the hedge as it curves round to a gate at the end of the orchard. Go through into a field and head towards footpath signs which lead you through a gate on the right boundary to Amhurst Bank Road.

Turn left along the road for about half a mile, passing Amhurst Hill Farm with its hoppers huts. Go downhill, cross a bridge and turn immediately right along a track through woods. Keep left along the fenceline and look for a gate if you wish to extend your walk to Pembury Old Church (20 minutes there and back), and the link with Walk 5. Otherwise skip to **Continuing Walk 4**.

To Pembury Old Church

Turn left through the gate into a field. Go directly across the fields using the stiles to guide you until you reach a gate into Old Church Road. Turn right for the church. Walk 5 begins here.

B

The knights walked this way and would have seen the beautiful golden sandstone nave of the church as it is today. The tower and roof were a little later (14th century). To the west of the church (left side if looking from the road), was Southfrith, part of the great hunting chase of the Clares and from here the knights followed the 'forest pale' south east to Tunbridge Wells.

Continuing Walk 4:

Continue through the wood, keeping alongside the fence on your left. At the end, turn right and keep to the main track which winds downhill with some steps to a plank footbridge and then go uphill and you will soon follow a fence on your left. Continue along the path high up above a small but steep valley. Arrive at a fence, climb over the stile and continue along the right side of a large field. Look for a waymarked post on your right and go over a stile into another field. Pass a pond and then turn left through a gate into a cherry orchard.

Continue along the left boundary and go over a stile into an apple orchard. Go straight ahead towards a pylon on the other side of the fence to your left and when you are level with it, bear right (looking out for waymarks) making your way to the right boundary marked by a row of silver birch trees. Turn left downhill and at the end of the orchard, go through a gate and continue along the right side of a field for about 100 metres. Turn right through a gate here (if there is one) and continue to another orchard. Go slightly right along a grass path between the rows of trees, then bear left towards buildings and go through to a drive. Emerge on Amhurst Bank Road, turn left and continue down and up the road.

When the road bends sharply left, keep straight ahead along a bridleway. Continue downhill towards Capel Church, passing old hoppers huts. Arrive at Alders Road, cross over to Church Lane and continue uphill past the church.

The church is well worth a visit if it is open, to see the 13th century wall paintings and the old yew tree in the churchyard. There are some benches dotted about for a good rest.

Pass Tanners Farm on your right and about 100 metres further on, turn right along a track and enter a large field. Turn left across a yard, go through a gate and bear right across the field (under power lines), towards a post in the far hedgeline. Go though a gate to Sychem Lane. Turn left and take the next right along a drive towards Lydd Farm. Before the Clock House, turn left over a stile into fields. Continue straight along the middle field and at the far end, turn right over a stile and follow an enclosed path, rejoining the route of the outward journey. Cross a footbridge and turn left continuing to Five Oak Green.

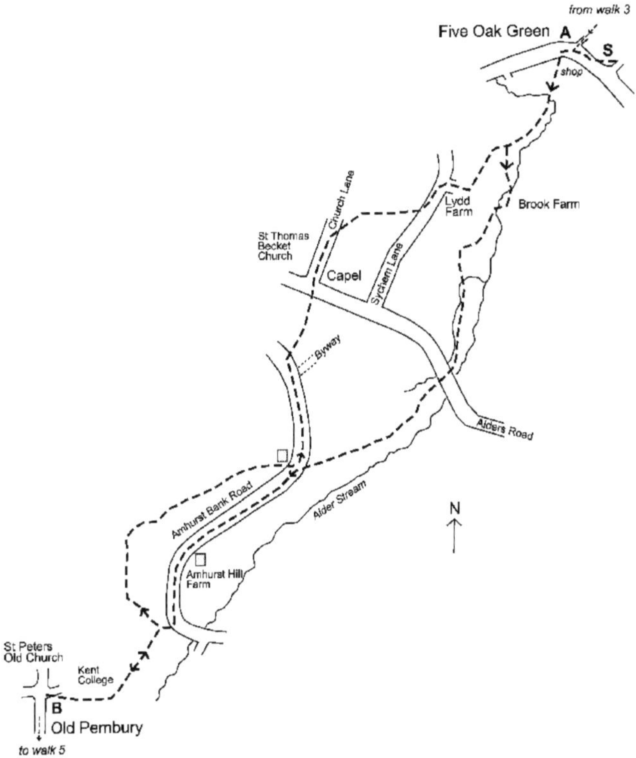
from walk 3
Five Oak Green
A
S
shop
Lydd Farm
Brook Farm
Church Lane
St Thomas Becket Church
Capel
Sychem Lane
Byway
Alders Road
Amhurst Bank Road
Alder Stream
N
Amhurst Hill Farm
St Peters Old Church
Kent College
B
Old Pembury
to walk 5

Walk No. 5

Old Pembury and Pembury Green

(by the pale of the forest)

Distance: 5.5 miles; OS Explorer 136
Start: Pembury Old Church (or Pembury Green, see page 26)

Mainly coppiced woods and orchards with some interesting buildings in Pembury. An off road alternative reduces the road walking along Pembury High Street.

A

From the church, walk down Old Church Road passing Kent college and then the waterworks. Cross Redwings Lane and continue up to the A228 Maidstone Road (Pembury By-Pass). At the junction follow the pavement round to the left and spiral uphill to cross the footbridge over the road. Go forward for a short distance on what used to be the continuation of Old Church Road and then turn right along a footpath, running parallel with the A288. Turn left in front of a gate and follow an enclosed path between high fences.

This long footpath follows the edge of the southern part of the Clares' hunting chase, called Southfrith. Here the knights were perambulating 'by the pale of the forest' and following the old parish boundary between Tonbridge and Pembury.

Continue on this woodland path and after a while pass a school and small graveyard on your left. A little further on, bear right across a plank bridge and continue ahead for about half a mile, ignoring paths to right and left. After a gate, you will emerge at the large road junction where Tonbridge Road becomes Pembury High Street.

This junction was once called Woodsgate, the site of an entrance into the Southfrith woods. The chase or forest (as the frith was sometimes called) wasn't necessarily wooded, but was likely to be a mix of woods, scrub and heath suitable for hunting.

Turn left onto Pembury High Street and continue for about half a mile to Pembury Green.

B

To return to Old Pembury, you can continue on the Hastings Road for about 500 metres until you reach Canterbury Road on your left, and rejoin the route at ****** page 27, or follow the off road directions below:

Off Road Route:

From the green cross the High Street and continue down Chalket Lane, on the left side of The Camden Arms. Continue through a pair of open white gates and in a short while, turn left on a narrow footpath immediately in front of the gateway to Great Bayhall House. Continue along in the same direction and in a while go through a fence and turn left, walking alongside the A21 road cutting on your right. Continue to the footbridge. If you wish to start Walk 6, cross over the footbridge, otherwise turn left through trees and then follow the left side of a field to the Hastings Road. Turn left then first right down Canterbury Road.

** Continue along Canterbury Road and at the T junction, turn right along Henwood Green Road, passing allotments on your left. Soon turn left down Woodside Road and then right up Henwoods Mount towards Woodside Playing Fields. At the end of the road keep left along a paved track, come to a gate and go through into the playing fields. Keep straight ahead along the right edge, and at the corner go over two stiles. Continue ahead into a field and shortly turn left following the Tunbridge Wells Circular Walk (TWC) along the left side of the field. Bear left to the corner and cross over a stile. Continue along the TWC, descending on a grassy path between fields. Cross a track and go straight along a narrow path, past a garden. Climb over a stile to Romford Road.

Turn left and continue uphill. At the crest, turn right along a track, called The Woodlands. Continue past houses and about 100 metres after the last one and before a large gateway ahead, turn left down a footpath (TWC), leading to Snipe Wood Farm. Continue along an enclosed track to a T junction, turn right and continue to a waymarked junction. Keep straight ahead along the main track and in a little while descend along a narrowing path to a four way finger post. Here the main track turns right, but keep straight ahead in the direction of TWC (Groombridge 13 miles) and proceed through woods on a narrow, winding and muddy path to a brick footbridge.

A mill once stood here. It was called Herrings Mill and may be the Pembury Mill painted by JMW Turner, although the location is still debated.

Continue uphill through orchards and arrive at a T junction. Turn left and continue for about 200m to an open grassy area with a wooden shelter. Look for a hidden footpath (TWC) on your right, next to a telegraph post. Turn right here, into an orchard at Pippins Farm. Continue along the left side and turn left along a track between the farm buildings, joining the long farm drive (passing Pippins Farm Shop), to Maidstone Road. Cross over and go straight along the opposite driveway and round to the right (following car park signs), to Downingbury Farm Shop.

Walk past the entrance and continue round the building, passing a pylon. Shortly you will reach a bridge on your right taking you over the Pembury By-Pass (TWC). At the end of the bridge go down steps on the left, through a gate and continue along the field edge. Go through another gate and turn right downhill towards the reservoir. Look out for a stile in the fenceline half way down, go through and bear right across the field to another gate. Go through and continue down to Redwings Lane. Turn left and at the junction with Old Church Road, turn right and continue back to St. Peters Old Church.

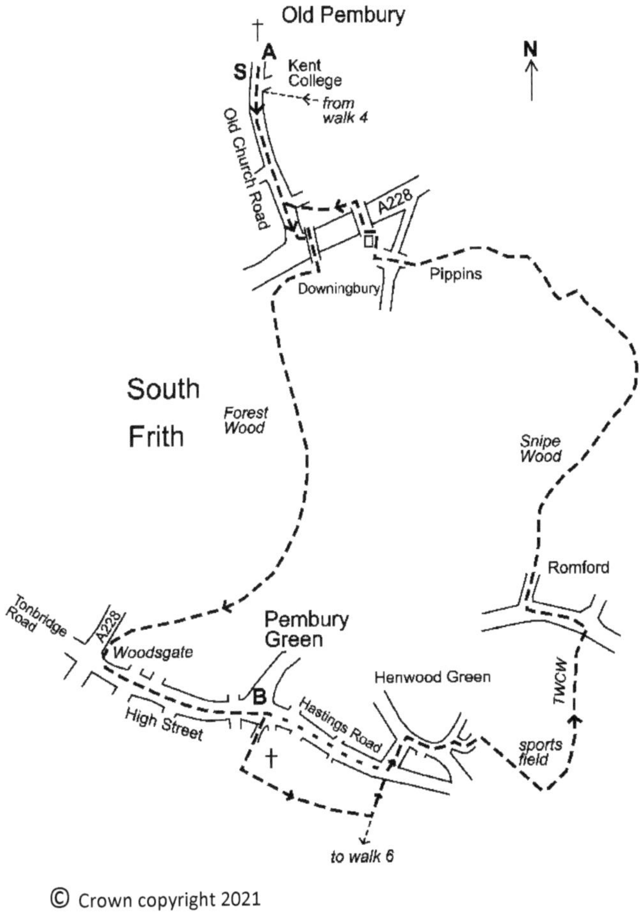
Old Pembury
A
S
Kent College
from walk 4
N
Old Church Road
A228
Pippins
Downingbury
South Frith
Forest Wood
Snipe Wood
Romford
Tonbridge Road
A228
Pembury Green
Woodsgate
Henwood Green
B
High Street
Hastings Road
TWCW
sports field
to walk 6

Walk No. 6

Pembury Green and Tunbridge Wells

(the pale of the forest to Bromelegeregg)

Distance: 7.5 miles; OS Explorer 136
Start: Pembury Green (or Tunbridge Wells, see page 33)

This route involves some road walking through the centre of Tunbridge Wells, linking green spaces and traffic-free roads as much as possible. The views from Pembury and along High House Lane are spectacular.

A

From the green, cross the High Street and continue along Chalket Lane, a no-through road on the left side of The Camden Arms. Continue through a pair of open white gates and when you reach the gateway to Great Bayhall House, turn left along a narrow footpath immediately in front. Continue in the same direction and in a while go through a fence and turn left, travelling alongside the A21 below on your right. Continue to the footbridge and cross over, now following the Tunbridge Wells Circular Walk (TWC).

Go straight on and then right, all the time following a high fence on your left. Leave the fence and continue ahead to a path junction with good views from a fieldgate. Turn right along a wide track and after about 100m, turn left over a stile into a field. Continue downhill with glorious views all round.

The route of the knights between Woodsgate and Tunbridge Wells (King Charles the Martyr Church) is uncertain but is likely to have been somewhere between your current route and the high ridge to your right, on which is Pembury Road (A264). Bromelegeregg is an old name used to describe the Tunbridge Wells area. It is likely to mean a ridge or high ground with open broom or heath type vegetation.

At the bottom of the hill, pass rough ground on your left and continue over a stile and a footbridge. Turn right along Chalket Lane and shortly take the next left along a wooded track (TWC). Arrive at a field and go uphill on the right side. Bear right along a narrow wooded path along the right edge of the field, and then emerge in the open again with a bank on your left. At the end, continue ahead onto High Woods Lane and pass some cottages on your right and then shortly go through the yard of Little Bayhall Farm.

Downhill on your left was once a grand country house called Bayhall, demolished in 1960. Long before, it was the site of a medieval moat house and the home of the Culpeper family. They may have taken part of their name from the old name of Pembury, Peppingeberia. More recent owners included the Amhurst and Camden families.

Continue along the lane for just over a mile with lovely views throughout, passing Mouseden Farm on your right and further on, TW Bowls Club. Here, the country lane turns into a residential road. Arrive at a T junction with Halls Hole Road, turn left and soon reach Bayhall/Forest Road. Keep left on the pavement, cross Dorset Road to a shop and continue on the busy Forest Road to the next island where you can cross over and join Camden Park, a no-through road. Continue along, the road narrowing to a path through light woodland and parkland. Emerge onto a road, turn right and after a few paces turn left along a restricted byway, passing two gateposts bearing the names 'Hollyshaw Close' and 'Fratton'.

Come out at Claremont School and bear right along a path between Glen Cottage and the school. Arrive at a T junction with Claremont Road, cross over and turn left. Pass Arundel, Norfolk, Grecian and Buckingham Roads on your right and then continue into Grove Park. Keep to the left side of the park and continue straight down the narrow, partially cobbled, street of South Grove. Emerge onto the High Street and turn left, continuing along a raised pavement. At the end, cross Mount Sion and go straight along a pedestrian street towards the church of King Charles the Martyr. Turn right, pass the church entrance and contnue round to the other side.

This 17th century church is well worth a visit. In the paving on the south side (right side of the church if you are facing the entrance), look for a three way boundary; Sussex to the south and the Kent parishes of Speldhurst and Tonbridge to the north. Another stone in the church wall, marks the boundary between Speldhurst and Tonbridge. At this point you are at the most southerly point of the old parish of Tonbridge, marking also the most southerly point of the Lowy of Tonbridge where the knights turned and headed back north.

B

Continue along the south wall of the church and go straight ahead along the brick path of Cumberland Walk. Arrive at a road, turn right and then shortly left along Upper Cumberland Walk which becomes a road. Pass the Lawn Tennis Club on your right and then keep left where the path significantly narrows alongside the Tunbridge Wells to Hastings railway line.

Cross over the railway via the footbridge and shortly arrive at Cavendish Drive. Turn right, pass Delves Avenue and continue to a mini roundabout. Turn right along Farmcombe Road and keep straight ahead at another mini roundabout, proceeding to the junction with Forest Road. Turn left and then right along Boundary Road. Come to a T junction and turn right along Hawkenbury Road.

Hawkenbury is recorded in the perambulation as 'hocubery'. It was claimed to be the king's land and therefore not in the Lowy of Tonbridge and had nothing to do with the Clares.

Cross Maryland Road, pass hockey pitches on your left and continue to a car park on your left. Just beyond, turn left onto a footpath signed, TWC/HWW. Follow a holly hedge on your left and pass a metal hurdle. Keep straight ahead ignoring paths to left and right although muddy conditions might lead to small diversions. Arrive again at High Woods Lane. Turn right and continue along the lane to the cottages at the end, where you meet two tracks. Take the right one into a field and then keep left (TWC), descending along the left edge of the field. At the bottom, keep straight ahead along a wooded track and reach a T junction. Turn left on this unmade section of Chalket Lane, ascend the hill and cross over the road bridge over the A21. Continue along Chalket Lane to Pembury Green.

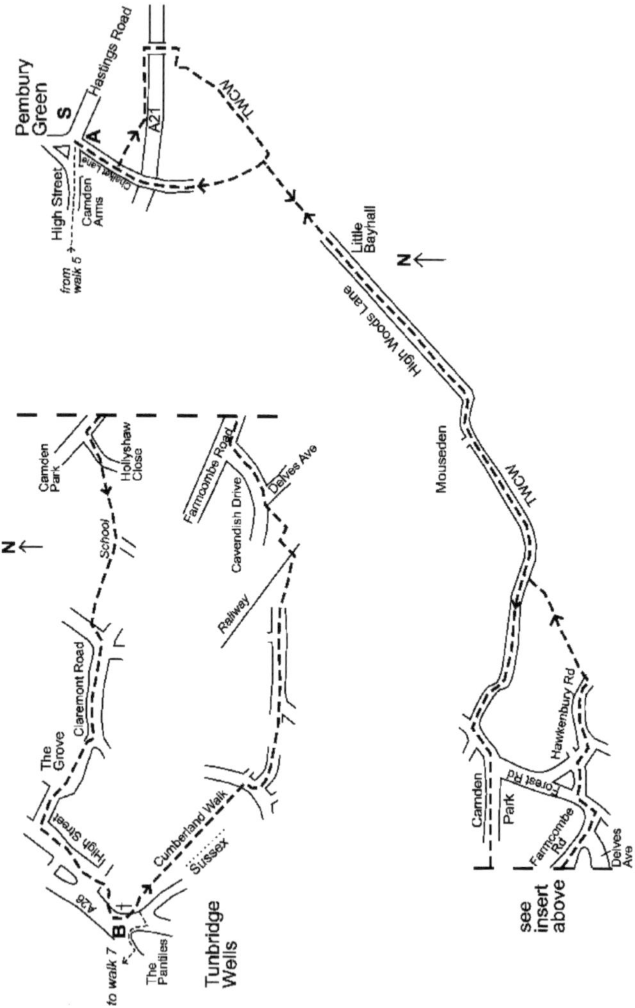
Pembury Green
S
Hastings Road
A
A21
TWCW
High Street
Camden Arms
Chalket Lane
from walk 5
Little Bayhall
N
High Woods Lane
Mouseden
TWCW
Hawkenbury Rd
Camden
Park
Forest Rd
Farmcombe Rd
Delves Ave
see insert above
Camden Park
Hollyshaw Close
Farmcombe Road
Delves Ave
Cavendish Drive
N
School
Railway
Claremont Road
The Grove
High Street
Cumberland Walk
Sussex
A26
B
to walk 7
The Pantiles
Tunbridge Wells

Walk No. 7

Tunbridge Wells and Stockland Green

(Bromelegeregg to the house of William Shrufin)

Distance: 6 mles; OS Explorer 147
Start: Tunbridge Wells (or Speldhurst, starting on Lower Green Road at the bottom of Speldhurst Hill, page 39)

This walk takes you through Tunbridge Wells and Rusthall Commons and through plenty of woodland. The roads through Tunbridge Wells are mainly quiet but you can choose a shorter and more off road route, avoiding Tunbridge Wells altogether, if you start from Speldhurst (go to page 39).

A

From the south side of the church of King Charles the Martyr, cross Nevill Street towards the Pantiles. Turn right and cross London Road to The Forum, (built as 'rest rooms' in 1939 and now a live music venue). Walk up the right side and at a T junction turn right and continue straight, ignoring paths to left and right, until you emerge again on London Road. Cross over at the island, turn left and then bear right along the red brick paving of Inner London Road, running parallel with the main road.

The red brick pavement is a feature of Tunbridge Wells and there will be more of it on todays walk. Long before the town's existance, the knights travelled this way, between the chase of

Southfrith, Tonbridge Parish, on your right and Speldhurst Parish on your left.

Continue to Mount Ephraim Road. Cross over and join Mount Ephraim (the main road). Cross over at the pelican crossing ahead, turn left and continue along the high road (still Mount Ephraim). Soon turn right down Royal Chase and continue straight.

This road takes you to the Culverden estate where Willelmi de Colverdene resided in 1279. From here and all the way to William Shrufin's house, near the top of Franks Hollow Road, you will follow the knights walk, almost exactly.

At the crossroads, cross Connaught Way and continue down Byng Road to a T junction. Turn right along Culverden Down and just before Coniston Avenue, turn sharp left down a footpath to a stream. Continue alongside the stream and emerge at the other end of Coniston Avenue. Cross over and go straight along a wide track past a waterworks on the left.

****** Continue ahead to a gate leading into Hurst Wood. Go through and fork right uphill. Keep straight ahead for a while to a gate. Climb over the stile and continue on an enclosed path and descend, keeping to the left path as you go. Cross a stream and go uphill on a steep narrow path to Broomhill Road. Turn right and shortly pass the entrance to Mill Farm Close. Cross a bridge and soon turn left, just before a high stone wall. Continue alongside the stream on this enclosed path and then steeply uphill between fields.

At the top, cross Speldhurst Road and continue ahead up stone steps and through a gate to join a narrow footpath. Arrive at a T junction and turn left on the Tunbridge Wells Circular Walk (TWC). Go through a gate to a field and bear right, joining the Weald Way (WW). Keep to the right side of the field, cross over a stile and continue along the edge of another field to Stockland Green Road. Turn left and pass Franks Hollow Road (the link with Walk 8).

B

Continue down Stockland Green Road to Forge House. Turn right through the tall metal gate and cross the drive. Proceed downhill on a footpath with steps to the former Speldhurst Mill, now houses. Following WW and TWC waymarks, continue along the drive to Speldhurst Hill and cross over. Turn left down the hill and next right along Lower Green Road. In about 100 metres, as the road bends left, turn right along a bridleway into Shadwell Wood.

Continue for about half a mile along this wide woodland track. You will reach a major junction where the TWC link route joins from the right. Shortly after, turn left up a bank and off the track, following the TWC link route. Soon go over a stile into a field and head directly across and over a stile in the top right corner. Continue along an enclosed path and join a wide track. Keep straight ahead and emerge on Lower Green Road in Rusthall. Cross over and turn right to The Red Lion pub with its lovely golden sandstone wall. Continue to the green and join a paved path to Rusthall Road. From here, either take the shorter route back to Speldhurst (described below), or skip to **Continuing Walk 7**.

Shorter, mainly off-road route, back to Speldhurst: Turn left and as you approach Bretland Road veer left on a path, cross the road and continue on the path downhill. Cross Rusthall Grange and on down to Apsley Street. Turn left and continue along Woodside Road and straight on along a footpath to a T junction with waterworks on your right. Turn left and continue from **** page 38.

Continuing Walk 7:
Cross over and bear left along a path across the common. You will arrive at the busy Langton Road. Continue ahead, cross Rusthall Road and pass the high stone wall of Tunbridge Wells Golf Club and then the Spa Hotel. At the junction with Major Yorks Road, cross over Langton Road to the former Major York pub and continue down the left side of the building on a paved footpath. Cross the entrance drive to Nevill Park, descend steeply and then go uphill and continue ahead, crossing Hungershall Park. Bear left across Tunbridge Wells Common and keep straight ahead until you arrive at a car park on your right, and then Major Yorks Road.

Cross over and turn right, then shortly bear left and continue to London Road. Cross over a pedestrian crossing and turn left towards the Church of King Charles the Martyr. Any of the passages on the right will lead you to the Pantiles where you can visit the chalybeate spring on which the growth of Tunbridge Wells was founded, in the 17th century.

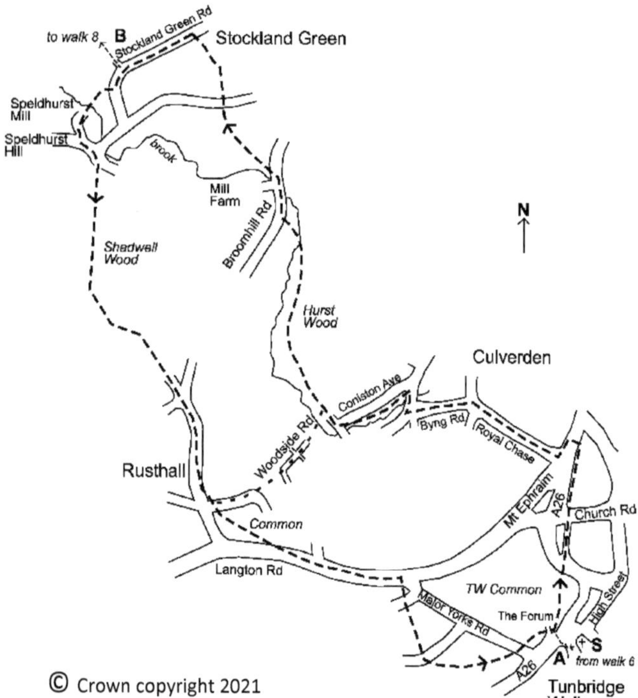

to walk 8
B
Stockland Green Rd
Stockland Green
Speldhurst Mill
Speldhurst Hill
brook
Mill Farm
Broomhill Rd
Shadwell Wood
Hurst Wood
N
Culverden
Coniston Ave
Byng Rd
Royal Chase
Woodside Rd
Rusthall
Mt Ephraim
A26
Church Rd
Common
Langton Rd
TW Common
Major Yorks Rd
The Forum
High Street
A
S
from walk 6
A26
Tunbridge Wells

Walk No. 8

Stockland Green and Poundsbridge

(the house of William Shrufin to Smethedonne)

Distance: 4.5 miles; OS Explorer 147
Start: Speldhurst Village

Hills, fields, bluebell woods, historic houses, an old iron production site and splendid views throughout.

Set off down Speldhurst Hill and towards the bottom, turn left along the drive of old Speldhurst Mill (now housing), following signs for the Weald Way (WW). Continue through the small estate, over a footbridge and uphill on the other side. Arrive at Forge House, go through a gate and turn left along Stockland Green Road. Continue uphill until you reach the junction with Franks Hollow Road.

A

Turn down Franks Hollow Road and pass the entrance to Scriventon House on your left. Continue more steeply downhill and where the road bends sharply right, turn left over a stile along a footpath and cross the field to the far left corner.

Scriventon House on your left, is the house of William Shrufin, passed by the knights in 1279. The English or Anglo-Saxon sc is pronounced sh and -ton (meaning place), is an addition.

Go over the stile, continue straight and over another stile. Bear right across a yard and climb over a stepped stile. Pass the barn on your right and continue downhill on a good track. At the bottom, cross a footbridge and bear right towards houses.

You are following the exact route of the knights and the Tonbridge boundary. The woods to the right are called Tonbridge Wood and to the left, Speldhurst Wood.

Continue on the track to a stile and follow a short residential road to Barden Road. Turn left and shortly turn right on the drive for Barden Furnace Farm. Pass a pond on your left and keep straight ahead along a sometimes muddy track and go over a stile.

Iron was manufactured at Barden Furnace in the Civil War for the parliamentary army but the industry is older than that. The ridge on your right as far as Penshurst is rich in iron and here in 1279, the knights named it 'smethedonne' (smiths hill). You will pass a series of ponds (some now dry) on your left which were used as heads of water to drive the mill for hammering iron.

Continue straight along the left side of several fields, passing ponds and woods on your left (there may be stiles or footbridges to cross on the way). After the last field, emerge on Penshurst Road at Poundsbridge.

B

Turn right to the junction and then left past an interesting Elizabethan house.

The initials WD stand for William Durkinghale. This family name is seen frequently in medieval documents relating to Penshurst and Chiddingstone (including the perambulation). The modern version of the name is Durtnall.

After the house, turn next right along Coopers Lane and continue to Hamsell Farm. Pass Little Colnbrook on your left and shortly after the houses, turn left on a public footpath. Bear right uphill through three fields, following signs. As a guide: first go through the right hedge towards the top; second, though the top hedge/fence at the centre; third, the top right hand corner. Go through a gate to Coopers Lane and turn left. Continue uphill to the junction with Poundsbridge Lane and cross over to join a public footpath opposite (WW). Go through a wooded area with ponds and cross over a stile on your left. Cross a field and go over another stile and then across another field towards the left corner and woodland. Go over a stile, turn left and proceed downhill through the wood, ignoring paths to the left and right.

Descend steeply to a stream and cross a footbridge, then go uphill on the other side. At the top, turn left in front of a house and garage (WW) and continue to Bullingstone Lane. Turn right and pass Bullingstone Farm and The Old Farmhouse on your left, then turn left at a footpath sign (WW). Continue in the same direction along this path, crossing a stile and keeping ahead towards houses. You will emerge on Penshurst Road at Speldhurst. For the centre of the village, turn right and follow the road round, passing the church on your left and the George and Dragon pub on your right. Continue down for Speldhurst Hill.

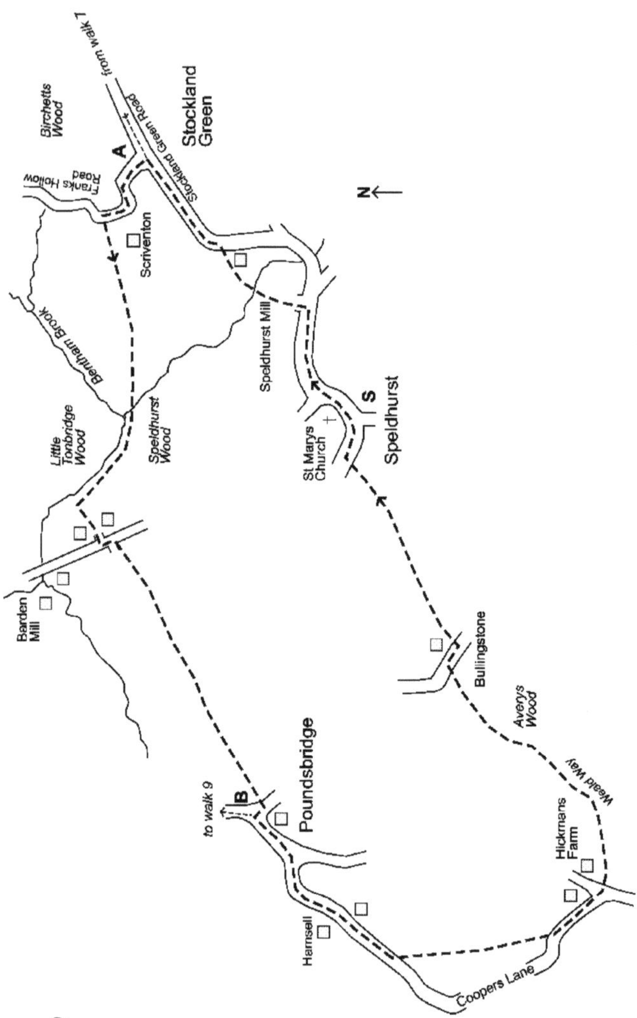
from walk 1
Stockland Green
Stockland Green Road
Birchetts Wood
A
Franks Hollow Road
N
Scriventon
Benthem Brook
Speldhurst Mill
S
Speldhurst
St Marys Church
Little Tonbridge Wood
Speldhurst Wood
Barden Mill
Bullingstone
Averys Wood
Weald Way
Poundsbridge
B
to walk 9
Hickmans Farm
Harmsell
Coopers Lane

Walk No. 9

Poundsbridge and Penshurst

(Smethedonne to the garden of Penecestr)

Distance: 3.5 miles; OS Explorer 147
Start: Penshurst Place or Village

Nearly all of this walk is along the wide Medway Valley with good views throughout and in the summer you may see swifts darting about in the meadows.

From the entrance of Penshurst Place, walk through the village passing the Leicester Arms and immediately after the school, turn right along The Warren. Continue until you reach Warren Farm and turn left here, along a public footpath. Keep alongside a hedge on your left and follow it round to a corner. Turn right and continue alongside houses. At a T junction, turn left along a track and keep straight ahead to Fordcombe Road. When you reach the road, turn right, but you may find a parallel path just off the road which is preferable. Either way, shortly cross over the road bridge (Long Bridge), on Fordcombe Road.

Immediately after the bridge, turn left down steps and cross a footbridge. Head directly across a field towards a house (Ford Place). As you approach, cross a track and follow a narrow path ahead through a small stand of trees and pass the entrance gate of the house. Continue ahead downhill along a treelined track. Cross over a ditch and keep directly ahead across a field to trees. The trees are concealing the River Medway and a pill box. Continue straight ahead, keeping to the left side of the fields and following the river on your left. You will come to a field corner where you turn right and follow the field edge to the next corner. Here, look for a gate on your left and go through into another field. Keep along the right edge of the field, following a fence down to a footbridge over the river.

Cross over and continue straight ahead across the field, soon following a ditch on your left and go through a gateway. Turn right and head straight uphill across the next field aiming towards a chapel (All Souls, Poundsbridge). Go through a gate on the left side of the chapel and continue to Coopers Lane. Turn left and then left again to reach the Elizabethan House at Poundsbridge (see note about the house on page 44).

A

Turn left at the T junction and continue along Poundsbridge Lane, passing Bowens Cottage and Bowens Farm. Soon turn left at the next public footpath just before a house and enter the drive. Go through a gateway ahead and continue along the right side of the field and through a gate to an enclosed path. Continue round to a T junction, turn right and bear left along a paved road through the small hamlet of Old Swaylands.

The knights passed through Bowen's Farm and Swaylands. It was called Swynesland in the 13th century, perhaps a Swineherd's land.

Shortly after Old Swaylands, a historic house with 15th century origins, turn left on a track just before another house, (the footpath sign may be hidden). Soon follow a high wall on your right. Go through a gate, continue along the right side of the field and keep ahead following this very good track which continues high above the Medway, to Penshurst. As you approach Penshurst you will have good views of the village. Arrive at a gate taking you onto Rogues Hill. Turn left, crossing over two bridges to Penshurst.

B

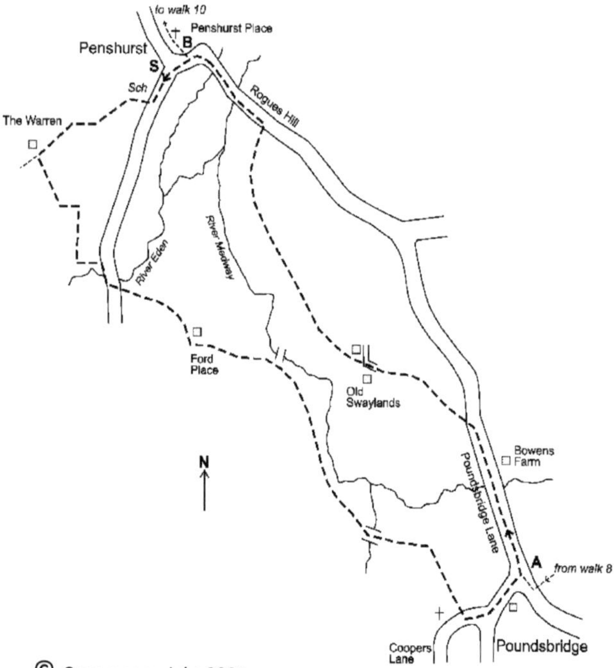

to walk 10
Penshurst Place
Penshurst
B
S
Sch
The Warren
Rogues Hill
River Eden
River Medway
Ford Place
Old Swaylands
N
Bowens Farm
Poundsbridge Lane
A
from walk 8
Coopers Lane
Poundsbridge

Walk No. 10

Penshurst and Chiddingstone Causeway

(the garden of Penecestr to Redelef)

Distance: 5.5 miles; OS Explorer 147
Start: Penshurst Place or Village

An Eden Valley round, through parkland, woods and pastures, with good views throughout.

A

Facing the village from Penshurst Place entrance, turn right up steps to pass through the picturesque buildings of 'Leicester Square' to the church.

Leicester Square is a pleasing mix of old 16th century and more recent 19th century buildings designed by George Devey, architect. There are some medieval features in the church and an effigy of Sir Stephen de Penecestre in chainmail (the Clares' most illustrious neighbour) lies on the floor of the Sidney Chapel. The jury of knights presented their findings to him, probably in the courtroom of Tonbridge Castle. At various times he was a king's justiciar, sheriff of Kent and lord warden of the Cinque Ports. He must have resided in a grand hall which preceded the more recent 14th century and later, Penshurst Place.

Continue past the church and go through a gate into Penshurst Park. Follow the wall on your right and where the path forks, bear slightly right towards a stand of conifers which you will shortly pass. Go through a gate ahead, cross the drive and through another gate. Continue ahead along the track through an avenue of trees, passing a cricket ground on your right. Follow the track as it bears right, leaving the avenue, to continue alongside it. Head for a gate ahead in the general direction of the house on the hilltop. Once through the gate, continue in that direction, straight uphill, leaving the main path on your right.

The knights came this way, after travelling through the garden of Penshurst and round the church. Penecestre was the 13th century name, the origins of which are unknown. The garden is not described, but it would have been a growing area for the household, vegetables or fruit trees, more what we would call a kitchen garden.

Keeping alongside a wood on your left, continue to the top left corner of the park. Just beyond the line of oaks there is a path leading left to a stile a few metres in from the corner. Cross over the stile and shortly over another, emerging at Redleaf Cottage and onto Penshurst Road. Turn right on this road and continue with care. It is not very busy but the traffic is fast.

This is the district of Redleaf (Redelef), through which the knights passed. The Durkinghale family resided here and the name is mentioned more than once in the route description.

Pass the grand entrance gate and old lodge of Redleaf House on your left. Continue on the road, passing a side road (signed to Penshurst Station). Just beyond, cross over where there is a green verge of sorts and in about 200 metres, turn left through a gate into Redleaf

Wood. Keep straight ahead as much as the winding path permits and descend gradually to a stream at the end of the wood.

Cross over the footbridge into a field and turn left through a gate, following the small stream on your left. Go through another gate and continue to the yard and converted buildings of Moorden Farm. Pass the barn on your left and turn left, then curve right along the track to Station Hill. Turn right and then, just after the oasts, fork left on a minor road which leads to Penshurst Station. You will arrive at a yard/car park, at the station. For Walk 11 cross over the footbridge to Chiddingstone Causeway. To continue on this walk, take the footpath on your left.

B

Follow the right side of the field and go through a gateway. Continue across the field to the far hedgeline. Turn left and continue along the field edge, alongside a stream. Look out for a waymarked field gate on your right and turn right here. Continue up the left side of the field, crossing over a stile or going through a gate into another field. Head up towards the oasts of Beckett's Farm and about half way up, turn left over a stile in the left fence.

Continue along the right side of the next field and pass through another field in the same direction. Continue to the corner and go through the gate. Bear slightly right across the next field towards a footbridge in the far right corner (don't be tempted by the field gate directly ahead). Cross over and go straight across the next field towards a gate on the far side. About half way across you will come alongside the Eden winding its way on your left. Go through the gate onto Hampkins Hill Road and turn left across Vexour Bridge. Go straight ahead off the road, between gateposts signed Vexour, and continue uphill along the entrance drive. Towards the top, turn right at the footpath sign and go up a scrubby bank into a field.

Turn left and continue along the left side of the field, passing buildings on your left. At the crest of the field, continue down on the left side and then bear right on a grassy path towards a house on the opposite side. Turn left just before the house and then turn right, immediately after it, continuing between buildings along the driveway to Wellers Town Road. Turn left and continue to Wellers Town. Cross over a bridge and go uphill passing rows of cottages. After the very last house, continue along the road and turn left at the first footpath sign.

Go over a stile and cross the field downhill in the direction of the very obvious building range on the opposite hill top. Keep alongside the broken tree line and bank which must have been a field boundary once. Cross a footbridge at the bottom and go through a gate. Go straight up the hill towards the left end of the buildings and go through a gate to a bridleway. The little hamlet here is called Wat Stock.

Turn left and continue downhill along the bridleway with good views of the Eden Valley and beyond. At the bottom, cross the bridge over the Eden and continue to Penshurst Road. Turn right to the junction and left to the entrance of Penshurst Place. If you are parked at Penshurst Place you can turn left at Penshurst Road and look our for a gate in the fenceline to the park. Go through and cross the park towards the church and on to Penshurst Place.

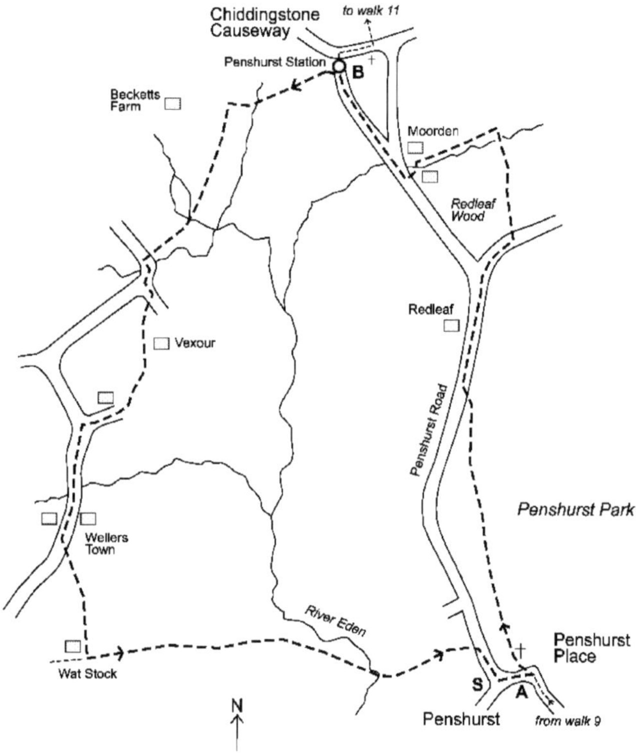

Chiddingstone
Causeway
to walk 11
Penshurst Station
B
Becketts
Farm
Moorden
Redleaf
Wood
Vexour
Redleaf
Penshurst Road
Penshurst Park
Wellers
Town
River Eden
Penshurst
Place
Wat Stock
S
A
Penshurst
from walk 9
N

Walk No. 11

Chiddingstone Causeway and Hale Oak

(Redelef to Coppingsland)

Distance: 5.5 miles or 4.5 miles; OS Explorer 147
Start: Penshurst Station, Chiddingstone Causeway

Pretty houses with red clay bricks and tiles are a feature of this walk which is mainly across fields, some of them surrounded by strips of woodland, called shaws. There is a reasonably quiet road option for a shorter return walk.

A

Starting at the front entrance of Penshurst Station, cross over the road to the Little Brown Jug, turn right and go uphill passing St. Lukes Church on your right. Shortly after, turn left on a footpath and continue on a paved path between fields to Camp Hill.

The field on your right used to be an airfield during the first half of the last century. In the 13th century this area was called herringsheath. You are following the knights route along the line of the Chiddingstone/Leigh Parish boundary.

When you meet the road, turn right and first left towards Charcott. Keep straight ahead, off the road, and along a track signed Charcott Farmhouse. Shortly turn right through a gate and then left across the field to a gate on the far side, passing the farm buildings on your left. Go through the gate and keep straight ahead, following a hedgeline on your left. From here you will be continuing in the same direction for some time

This hedge follows the parish and lowy boundary along which the knights walked, towards Coppings Land. Over to your right you will see Wickhurst Farm. Coppings Farm, which still bears the 13th century name, is beyond and a bit further away to your right.

At the end of the hedgeline, descend on a grassy track to Wickhurst Brook. Cross over the footbridge, continue uphill and rejoin the left hedge/boundary. Go through a gap in the field corner and continue straight ahead alongside the hedgeline. When the hedge runs out, keep straight ahead and continue past a small wood and pond on your right. Cross a footbridge, turn right and almost immediately left uphill, keeping alongside the field boundary on your left. This route is a slight deviation from the OS public right of way, so it could change, but any change will be insignificant.

Arrive at a clump of trees, concealing a pond. Skirt round it and then turn right along the hedgeline for about 100 metres to a gate. Go through and head straight across the next field, then follow an enclosed path with a lake on your right. Continue towards buildings and keep straight on, off the track, along a narrow enclosed and often muddy footpath, to emerge on Hale Oak Road. Go to **Continuing Walk 11** on the next page or follow the shorter road return below.

Shorter Road Return:

Here you can shorten the walk (or avoid further mud) by turning left along this generally quiet road for about a mile. Ignore the first footpath on your left at Little Hale and take the second on your left through a gateway into a field. Continue the directions at ****** on the next page.

Continuing Walk 11:

Turn right along the road for about 500 metres and pass a public footpath sign leading into a field on your right. This path is the link with Walk 12.

B

To continue Walk 11, turn left shortly at a footpath sign, just before a house. Cross over a small footbridge and go through a gate. Continue on the right side of the field, then straight downhill to a stream. Cross over a footbridge and stile and then go uphill and straight across the next field. Cross over a footbridge and another field. Go through a gate, cross a track and through another gate. Continue on a good path across the next field, passing to the right of a clump of trees, hiding a pond.

Continue through this very large nut nursery and go through a gate, cross straight over a track and cross over a footbridge. Turn right and follow the field edge alongside woodland. Maintain direction and cross the field to a corner. Go over a stile and a footbridge and continue along the field edge with the wood again on your right. Keep ahead along an enclosed path and emerge into a large field.

Bear left across the field towards a waymarked post next to a telegraph pole on the far side. Go through the gap in the boundary and turn right along a grassy track. Look for a gap on your left and turn here towards a footbridge over a stream. Cross over and then go up steps to a field. Head across the field on a left diagonal towards a brick structure which will soon come into view. Go through a gap in the fence and pass the building on your left, then turn right and continue round farm buildings to Bayleys Hill.

Turn left, pass the entrance to a house (Sharps Place) and then turn immediately left, up a bank and over a stile. Pass an oast on your left and continue ahead to another gate and go over the stile. Continue straight through fields and gates and then an enclosed and more wooded path with a pond on your left.

Arrive at a wood and turn left through this belt of trees to a field. Initially keep to the left side of the field and when the boundary swings left, cross straight ahead and go through a gate to Hale Oak Road. Turn right and then immediately left on a footpath through a gateway.

****** Go straight across the field passing Brownings Farm over on the right. Continue across the next field, bearing right to the corner. Go though a woodland track to a field and turn right keeping alongside the wood. Go through a gap and cross the next field towards a gate in the far left corner. Go through and continue along the left side of another field. At the next corner, go through a gate and head slightly left across this large field towards the left side of the buildings ahead of you.

Go through a waymarked gate into the driveway and turn left to the road. Turn left towards Charcott and shortly turn right to rejoin the path heading towards St Lukes Church. At the road, Turn right for Penshurst Station and Chiddingstone Causeway.

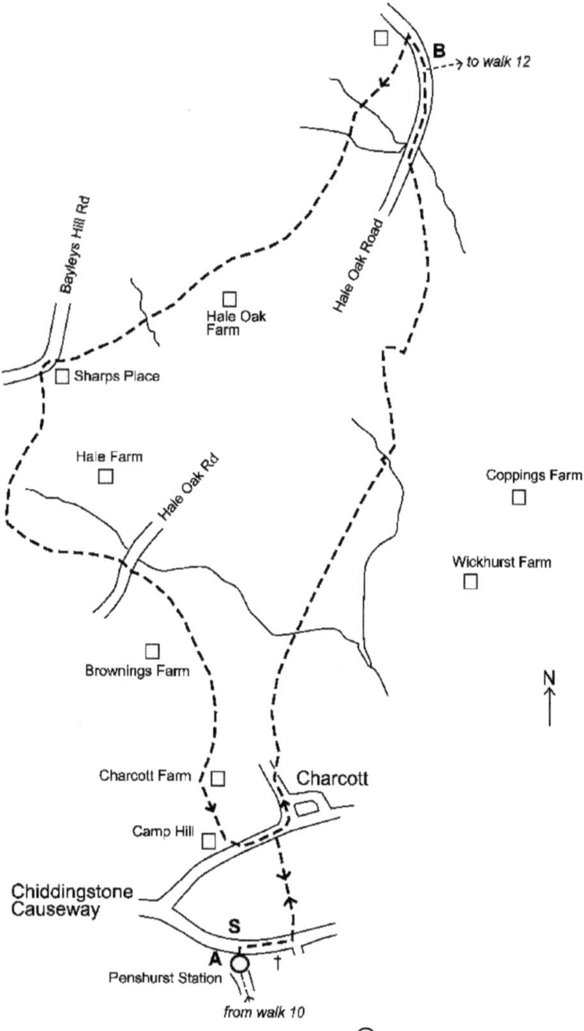
B
to walk 12
Bayleys Hill Rd
Hale Oak Road
Hale Oak
Farm
Sharps Place
Hale Farm
Hale Oak Rd
Coppings Farm
Wickhurst Farm
Brownings Farm
N
Charcott Farm
Charcott
Camp Hill
Chiddingstone
Causeway
S
A
Penshurst Station
from walk 10

Walk No. 12

Hale Oak and Weald

(Coppingsland to the mead of Nizels)

Distance: 2.5 miles; OS Explorer 147
Start: Memorial Village Hall, Weald Green

A short walk through pleasant woodland paths, pastures and meadow. Mostly level walking with just one gentle hill.

Pass the village hall on your right, towards the lower end of the green and continue downhill along a paved footpath, between houses, to Mount Pleasant Road. Turn right, pass a private road and shortly turn right again along a byway. Continue on this pretty broad track through woodland until you come to Hale Oak Road. Turn left and shortly left again through a stile leading into a field.

A

Go through and keep straight across the field to a footbridge. Cross over and climb up steps to a gate. Go through and cross the next field uphill, passing a telegraph pole. Go through a waymarked gate, cross the farm track and through another gate. Continue along the left side of the field, through a gate and then through another field and gate onto a track alongside a garden to Scabharbour Road, Fletchers Green.

Turn left and then right down Eggpie Lane, shortly reaching a footpath on your left (the sign may be hidden). Go through the gate and keep to the right side of a this long field, passing through a gap in a fence about half way. Aim for the far left corner and go over a stile. Turn right and follow the hedge on your right, continuing through a gap to the next field. Head straight across and through a gate and then across a shorter field. Arrive at the gate opposite (Walk 13 can be joined from here).

On the other side of the gate to your right (behind the fence) is an old parish boundary stone. Tonbridge, Leigh and Weald Parishes all meet here. It marks a northern boundary of the Lowy of Tonbridge with Weald and Sevenoaks Parishes on the outside and Leigh and Tonbridge within, The knights must have passed here too. The low lying fields you have just come across are likely to have been part of the 'mead of Nizels', in 1279.

B

Go through the gate, if you are not there already, and proceed along the right side of this field to another gate and then follow the short track to Morleys Road. Turn left and in about 100 metres, take a footpath on your right, opposite Elses Farm entrance (it leads towards a sports ground).

Follow a wide, then narrow track, always keeping left through the woodland (this off road section is about half a mile in total). Arrive at Glebe Road and turn left to the crossroads. Turn right along Windmill Road and continue past Mount Pleasant Road, Elmsfield Close and The Windmill pub. Turn left after the pub along a paved path to the other side of the green where you will find the village hall and car park.

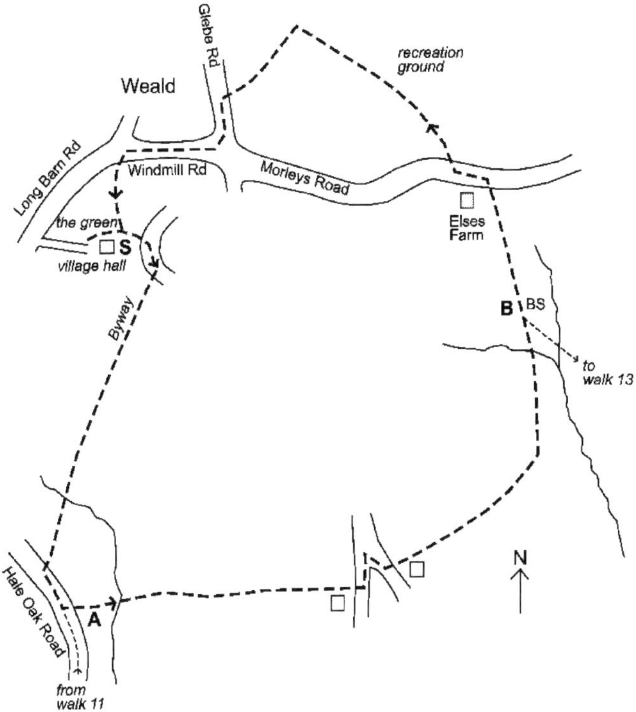

Glebe Rd
Weald
recreation ground
Long Barn Rd
Windmill Rd
Morleys Road
Elses Farm
the green
S
village hall
Byway
B
BS
to walk 13
N
Hale Oak Road
A
from walk 11

Walk No. 13

Weald and Underriver

(mead of Nizels to Romshedde)

Distance: 6.5 miles; OS Explorer 147
Start: Weald Green (or Underriver, see page 70)

There is some walking on pavements alongside the London Road B245, but it can be avoided by splitting the walk into two, one starting from Weald and retracing steps from the top of Nizels Golf Course, 3 miles in total; the other starting from Underriver (top of page 70) and walking to Romshed and back in a short circular, 2 miles.

From the top of Weald Green, turn right along Windmill Road to the crossroads. Here you can follow an off road route or continue straight along Morleys Road to Elses Farm.

Off Road Route:
Turn left along Glebe Road then right on a woodland footpath after The Wickets. Keep right, near to the edge of the woods, for about half a mile. Join a wider track to Morleys Road, opposite Elses Farm.

Both Routes:
With Elses Farm on your right, turn next right at a footpath sign. Continue along a short track and through a gate into a field. Keep straight along the left side of the field to the next gate, where there is an old parish boundary stone over the left fence.

A note about the boundary stone can be found on page 64. The low lying and damp meadows in front of you are likely to be the 'mead of Nizels' through which the knights walked.

A

Once through the gate, bear left across the field towards a gap in the corner. Continue left and cross over a footbridge into the next field. Walk across the field parallel with the railway line on your left, and towards the end, turn left through a gate and then a tunnel beneath the railway.

Emerge on Nizels Golf Course, go forward and pass Hole 3 on your left, continuing on a narrow path to a waymarked post. Turn right and continue uphill alongside a wood on your left. At the end of the wood, keep straight across the golf course, pass a pond on your left and go through to Nizels Lane. Turn left along a narrow and then wider lane passing Nizels on your left. Continue across the road bridge over the A21 and arrive at London Road.

The knights crossed this very old road and the 13th century description indicates a 'paved way'. In keeping with this enhanced status, it was the first turnpike road in Kent, opened in 1709.

Turn left and cross over to the pavement on the right side. Pass Bank Lane on your right and then the café on your left to Morleys roundabout.

Morleys Roundabout is named after a farm of that name close by. The café started life as Morleys Farm Hut, selling teas and farm produce. Lord Johannis de Morlay was one of four local lords who made up the jury along with 20 knights on this walk. Perhaps he was connected with this place and like the other lords and knights was chosen for his local knowledge of the area.

Continuing along London Road, pass St. Julian's Cottage on your right and just before the next house (St. Julian's Lodge), turn right into a driveway and walk through to a field gate. This restricted byway takes you for about half a mile through pleasant woods and then farmland. Just before a wood, turn right through a gate to Romshed Farm.

****** Once through the gate, go along the left side of the field to the end and turn left to a gateway. Climb over the stile and cross the field towards the right side of the farm buildings. At the corner, go over the stile, cross the drive and over another stile. Turn left across the field towards a pond and a field gate.

The pond is on the site of an old moat which once surrounded a medieval house. The knights passed through Romshed which has kept its name since at least the 13th century. St Julians House and lodges etc. are all part of this large estate, once called Romshedde Manor.

Climb over a stile by the gate and another stile ahead of you. Go straight on uphill and at a gate, go through and follow an enclosed path. Soon turn right, following the fence round and pass through a wooded area to a recreation ground. Keep along the right side to the corner and go over a stile to Carters Hill at Underriver.

B

Turn left and continue up Carters Hill, passing the White Rock Inn and village sign and on to a crossroads. Turn left along the bridleway and pass Black Charles on your right.

This name appears as early as the 14th century as a family name, Blakecherl, meaning dark man.

Continue uphill, arrive at a path junction and go straight on, soon passing Kettleshill Farm on your right. Continue, and after The Coach House on your right, turn left along a restricted byway. When you reach the small lake on your right, you will be able to see St Julians House beyond.

Now a private members' club, the house was built early in the 19th century by the Herries family who owned Romshed Manor.

Continue along the byway and after a wood on your left, pass the gate for Romshed Farm. If you would like to return to Underriver, turn left here and continue directions from ****** on the previous page. To return to Weald, you need to retrace your steps of the outward journey. As a reminder, keep straight on and come to London Road. Turn left and continue to Bank Lane, then turn right along Nizels Lane. Cross the road bridge over the A21 and pass Nizels on your right.

Continue along the single track road and at a left bend, take the first public footpath on your right. Bear right alongside a pond and then straight ahead across the golf course following signs. Descend on a track alongside a wood on your right. When the track curves left, keep straight ahead to the right of the tee and continue to a T junction. Turn left passing Hole 3 and continue ahead through the tunnel beneath the railway and into a field. Turn right following the railway and then aim for the far left corner of the field. Cross a footbridge and keep right into another field.

Bear left across the next field towards a gate opposite (the second gate from the right), go over the stile and continue along the right side of this field. Go through a gate and continue along a track to Morleys Road. Turn left and then next right for a footpath back to Windmill Road (keep left through the woods and then left along Glebe Road) or continue along Morleys Road to the crossroads and then on along Windmill Road to the green.

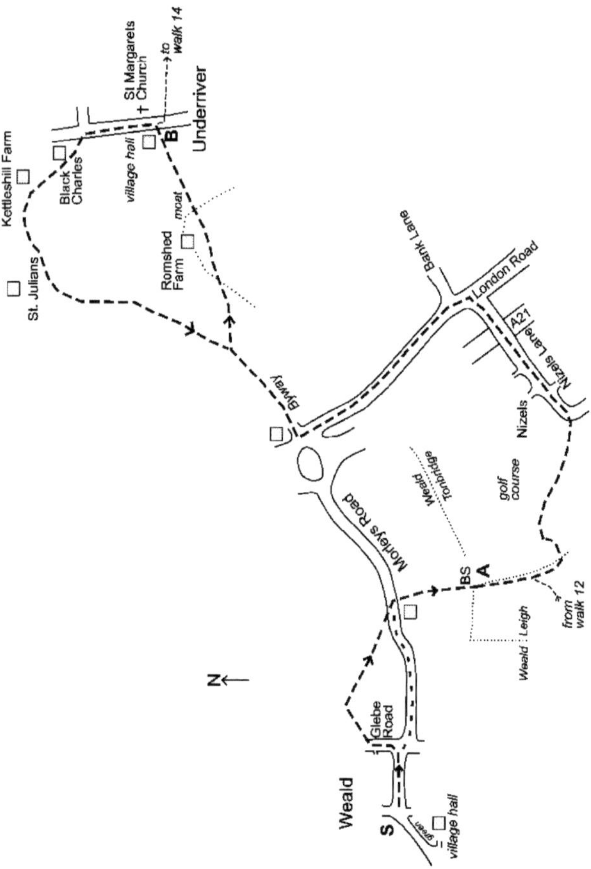

Kettleshill Farm
St. Julians
Black Charles
village hall
St Margarets
+ Church
to walk 14
B
Underriver
moat
Romshed Farm
Byway
Bank Lane
London Road
A21
Nizels Lane
Nizels
golf course
Weald
Tonbridge
Morleys Road
BS
A
from walk 12
Weald
Leigh
N
Glebe Road
Weald
S
green
village hall

Walk No. 14

Underriver and Shipbourne

(Romshedde to Somegate by the forest pale)

Distance: 5.5 miles; OS Explorer 147
Start: Underriver (or Shipbourne, see page 75)

Pleasant pastures and bluebell woods with a backdrop of the greensand ridge rising steeply to the north.

A

From Carters Hill, Underriver, pass the church on your left and after The Old Vicarage, turn left along a track. Continue straight and go through a gate into a field, then bear right to cross a footbridge into the next field. Keep left through a line of oak trees to the field corner and go over a stile.

This wide restricted byway has the appearance of a once important road linking Underriver with Shipbourne.

Continue in the same direction through an avenue of oaks and through two gates or stiles. Cross a large field on the left side to the next corner. Go over a stile to Underriver House Road. Turn right and follow the road for about a quarter of a mile. Turn left over a stile at the first footpath sign, just before a house. Bear left across the field and cross a stile in the next hedge. Turn right and head across the next field towards a row of houses. Join a paddock fence on your right and towards the end, turn right over a stile. Cross the field and go over a stile opposite. Turn left across a footbridge and continue along the track, passing Grenadier Cottages, to Riding Lane.

The houses were named after a pub called The Grenadier. It is marked on 19th century maps but was flattened by a bomb in 1942. After Riding Lane, the walk begins to follow the northern edge of North Frith, along the pale of the forest to Somegate.

Turn right past Gardener Hope Cottages and in a short while take the next footpath on your left along a drive leading to Fairhill. Continue between laurel hedges, passing Fairhill and soon leave the drive and continue straight ahead through a gateway on an uphill track through woodland. From this point you will be walking in the same direction for some time, (as you follow the pale of the 'northern forest').

At the end of the wood continue along an enclosed path alongside a field. Go over a stile, cross a bridge and over another stile, then continue ahead and over the next stile. Now go through a small wood and then the left side of a field, passing the buildings of Tinley Lodge Farm over on your right. Continue to the driveway. Turn left and then very soon turn right through a wood. Continue through this pine plantation and then along an enclosed path to a driveway with a house on your left. Continue forward to a path junction and fork left, following the path between fields to Hildenborough Road.

B

The 18th century historian, Edward Hasted, placed Somegate, (the start and end of the perambulation) on his local map, in this area of Shipbourne, called West Green.

Cross over and turn right along a wide grass verge. Shortly turn left across a footbridge and go directly across the field to the corner of a wood. Continue alongside the wood on your left, then keep ahead across the field and turn right across a ditch and uphill towards the church. At the other side of the field, turn left to the corner and the churchyard at Shipbourne. You can return to Underriver by turning left here and following the hedgeline across the field but if you want to visit Shipbourne, turn right into the churchyard and continue past the church towards the road and inn.

From the back gate of the churchyard at Shipbourne, follow the hedgeline on your right across the field. Go through a gap and continue uphill towards the corner of a wood. Climb over the stile into the wood and continue on a wide path. At a path junction, fork left uphill and continue more or less in the same direction, ignoring paths left and right, until you emerge on Mote Road at Budds Green. Turn left and then right along a restricted byway across the small green, keeping on the right side of Great Budds House.

Follow an enclosed path, passing a barn on your left and then a pond. Arrive at a field gate, go over the stile and head straight across the field along a stony track and across the next field in broadly the same direction.

Cross a footbridge and then a stile and another stile opposite. Keep straight ahead along the right side of the field towards a barn. Cross a yard with the barn on your right. Go across two stiles or through two gateways into the next field. Keep to the right side of the field, alongside a wood, and continue towards Underriver House. At the next corner go over a stile and turn right. Continue straight to a waymarked gate and turn left just before it, round the back of a boundary hedge. Follow the track and continue past cottages to Underriver House Road.

Turn left, pass a pond on your right opposite Underriver House, then shortly turn right over a stile at a footpath sign. Cross a footbridge into a field and continue ahead into the next field. Go directly uphill towards an oak tree and over a stile just beyond. Continue straight across two more fields and a further field with a treelined boundary ahead. Aim for the right side of the boundary and continue alongside a line of poplars to a gate in the field corner. Follow a short enclosed path to another gate and emerge on Carters Hill in Underriver. Turn left for the church and centre of the village.

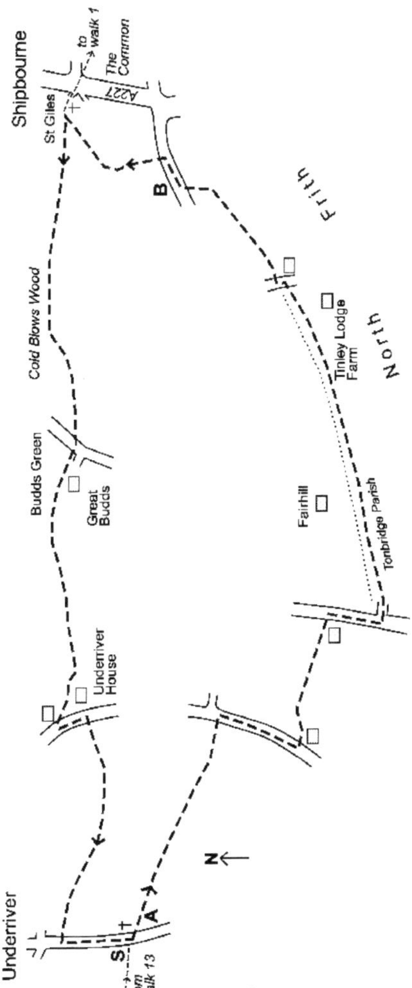
Shipbourne
St Giles
to walk 1
The Common
A227
B
Frith
North
Tinley Lodge Farm
Cold Blows Wood
Budds Green
Great Budds
Fairhill
Tonbridge Parish
Underriver House
N
Underriver
S
A
from walk 13